# Cool Hotels
## Germany

teNeues

# Imprint

Produced by fusion publishing GmbH, Stuttgart . Los Angeles   www.fusion-publishing.com

Editorial team: Martin Nicholas Kunz (Editor + Layout), Margareta Auer (Layout)
Bärbel Holzberg (Introduction), Patrice Farameh ("What's special" texts)
Katharina Feuer, Viviana Guastalla, Anne-Kathrin Meier (Editorial coordination)
Sabine Scholz (Text coordination), Alphagriese (Translation coordination French, English): Stéphanie Laloix (French),
Christine Grimm (US-English); Federica Benetti, Romina Russo (Italian), Sylvia Lyschik, Sergio Ramos Ramos (Spanish)
Everbest Printing Co.Ltd - www.everbest.com, Jan Hausberg (Prepress + imaging)

Cover photo (location): Gerbermühle, www.designhotels.com (Gerbermühle)

Back cover photos from top to bottom (location): East Hamburg, Doug Snower (East), Roland Bauer (Adlon Kempinski), Ackselhaus, Chris Valentin (Ackselhaus), Dieter Roosen (The Pure), courtesy Bayerischer Hof (Bayerischer Hof)

Photos (location): Ackselhaus, Chris Valentin (Ackselhaus), ArabellaStarwood Hotelpool GmbH (Sheraton Pelikan
Hotel), Becker's Hotel & Restaurant, www.designhotels.com (Becker's Hotel & Restaurant), Bernd Eidenmueller
(Der Zauberlehrling), Christian Perl (Superbude), courtesy Bayerischer Hof (Bayerischer Hof), courtesy Cerês (Cerês),
courtesy Cortiina (CORTIINA), courtesy Hotel de Rome (Rocco Forte Hotel de Rome), courtesy Hotel La Maison
(Hotel La Maison), courtesy Designhotel ÜberFluss (Hotel ÜberFluss), courtesy Mövenpick Frankfurt (Mövenpick
Frankfurt), courtesy Gastwerk (Gastwerk), courtesy HOPPER Hotel St. Antonius (Hotel St. Antonius), courtesy Hotel
Adlon Kempinski Berlin (Adlon Kempinski), courtesy Kempinski Grand Hotel Heiligendamm (Kempinski Grand Hotel
Heiligendamm), courtesy Kloster Hornbach (Kloster Hornbach), courtesy Madison Hotel (Madison Hotel Hamburg),
courtesy Mandarin Oriental, Munich (Mandarin Oriental, Munich), courtesy Mauritzhof (Mauritzhof), courtesy
The Mandala Hotel (THE MANDALA HOTEL), courtesy Villa Orange (Villa Orange), Dieter Roosen (The Pure), East
Hamburg, Doug Snower (East), Gavin Jackson (Ackselhaus, Hotel Q!), Gerbermühle, www.designhotels.com (Gerber-
mühle), Goldman 25hours, www.designhotels.com (Goldmann 25h), Jörg Tietje (Clipper Elb-Lodge, Monopol Hotel,
YoHo—the young hotel), Klaus Frahm, Side (Side), Martin Nicholas Kunz, Michelle Galindo (Riehmers Hofgarten,
Honigmond), Mövenpick Hotel Hamburg (Mövenpick Hotel Hamburg), www.guenterstandl.de (Hofgut Hafnerleiten)
All other photos by Roland Bauer

Price orientation: € = < 200 €, €€ = 201 – 350 €, €€€ = 351 – 550 €, €€€€ = > 551 €


Published by teNeues Publishing Group

teNeues Verlag GmbH + Co. KG        teNeues Publishing Company        teNeues Publishing UK Ltd.
Am Selder 37                        16 West 22nd Street                P.O. Box 402
47906 Kempen, Germany               New York, NY 10010, USA            West Byfleet
Tel.: 0049-(0)2152-916-0            Tel.: 001-212-627-9090             KT14 7ZF, Great Britain
Fax: 0049-(0)2152-916-111           Fax: 001-212-627-9511             Tel.: 0044-1932-403509
E-mail: books@teneues.de                                               Fax: 0044-1932-403514

teNeues France S.A.R.L.
93, rue Bannier
45000 Orléans, France
Tel.: 0033-2-38541071
Fax: 0033-2-38625340

Press department: arehn@teneues.de
Tel.: 0049-(0)2152-916-202

www.teneues.com

ISBN: 978-3-8327-9247-3

Bibliographic information published by Die Deutsche Bibliothek.
Die Deutsche Bibliothek lists this publication in the Deutsche Nationalbibliografie;
detailed bibliographic data is available in the Internet at http://dnb.ddb.de.

# Contents                              Page

Introduction                            5

# Einleitung

Zwischen der Nordseeküste und den Alpengipfeln im Süden gibt es vieles neu zu entdecken. *Cool Hotels Germany* ermöglicht einen ungewohnten Blick auf das Land im Herzen Europas und seine große Vielfalt, die sich in den sechzehn Bundesländern mit ihrem kulturellen Eigenleben und ihren charakteristischen Landschaften zeigt. Da sind zum Beispiel die Zeugen der Vergangenheit: die Burgen am Rhein, so gut erhalten, dass ein stattlicher Ritter jederzeit durchs Tor reiten könnte, die Schlösser und die mittelalterlichen Städte mit ihren sorgsam gepflegten Fachwerkhäusern. Oder die mäandernden Flussläufe, die ausgedehnten Wälder der Mittelgebirge und die blendend weißen Ostseestrände. Deutsche Seelenlandschaften, die Künstler zu Werken von Weltrang inspirierten. Vom Romantiker Caspar David Friedrich bis zu Gerhard Richter, einem der höchst gehandelten Künstler unserer Zeit. Ein Land voller Kleinode also, denen nachzuspüren sich lohnt.

In den Städten wie Hamburg, Düsseldorf, Köln, Frankfurt oder München signalisieren architektonische Highlights den Aufbruch ins 21. Jahrhundert. Und Berlin befindet sich auf dem besten Weg, sämtlichen Metropolen dieser Welt den Rang als coolste Stadt abzulaufen. Deshalb stellt *Cool Hotels Germany* gleich acht Adressen in der deutschen Hauptstadt vor. Auch Hamburg hat in puncto Coolness einiges zu bieten. Das *YoHo* hinter einer hanseatisch weißen Fassade gewährt allen Gästen unter 26 Jahre Rabatt. München mit seinen drei Pinakotheken bietet mit dem *La Maison* ein französisch anmutendes Hotel, von dem aus es nur wenige Schritte zum Englischen Garten und dem berühmtesten aller Biergärten am Chinesischen Turm sind.

Manchmal finden sich die coolen Hotels aber gerade dort, wo man sie am wenigsten erwartet. Im *Kloster Hornbach* an der französischen Grenze umfängt den Gast meditative Ruhe, sobald er hinter die Klostermauern tritt. In Trier, einst bedeutsame Stadt im Westen des Römischen Reiches, überzeugt das *Becker's Hotel* mit einem superstylischen Ambiente. Und eingebettet in die sanfte Landschaft des Bodensees hat eine Künstlerin mit dem *Schloss der Künste* ein besonderes – und erschwingliches – Refugium geschaffen. Mit diesem Führer im Gepäck auf Deutschlandreise zu gehen, bedeutet, den Blick zu schärfen, und oft genug auch, scheinbar Vertrautes aus einem neuen Blickwinkel wahrzunehmen.

Bärbel Holzberg

## Introduction

The area between the coast of the North Sea and the peaks of the Alps in the south offers many new discoveries. *Cool Hotels Germany* allows you an unusual look at the country in the heart of Europe while presenting the great variety of the sixteen German states, each with their own cultural life and characteristic landscapes. These include the witnesses of the past: the fortresses on the Rhine that are so well-preserved that an imposing knight could ride through the gate at any moment, the castles, and the medieval cities with their well-tended half-timbered houses. Or the meandering courses of the rivers, the extensive forests of the low mountain ranges, and the dazzling white beaches of the Baltic. These are landscapes of the German soul that have inspired artists to create world-class works that range from the Romantic painter Caspar David Friedrich to Gerhard Richter, who is one of the most highly traded artists of our age. A search for this country's gems will be richly rewarded.

In cities such as Hamburg, Düsseldorf, Cologne, Frankfurt, or Munich, architectural highlights signal the new departure into the 21$^{st}$ century. And Berlin is on the best path to overtaking all of the world's metropolises as the coolest city. This is why *Cool Hotels Germany* presents a total of eight addresses in the German capital alone. Hamburg also has a fair amount to offer when it comes to coolness. The *YoHo* behind a Hanseatic white facade guarantees a discount for all of its guests under 26. Munich with its three Pinakothek art galleries offers the French-inspired *La Maison* hotel, just a few steps away from the English Garden and the most famous of all beer gardens at the Chinese Tower.

But sometimes the cool hotels can be found where you least expect them. At *Kloster Hornbach* (Hornbach Monastery) on the French border, guests are surrounded by meditative peace as soon as they step behind the monastery walls. In Trier, which was once a significant city in the western Roman Empire, the *Becker's Hotel* convinces guests with its super-stylish ambience. And an artist has created a special—and affordable—refuge tucked away in the gentle landscape of Lake Constance with her *Schloss der Künste* (Castle of the Arts). Taking a trip through Germany with this guide in your luggage means sharpening your eyes, as well as frequently perceiving the seemingly familiar from a new perspective.

Bärbel Holzberg

# Introduction

Entre la côte de la Mer du Nord et les pics des Alpes au sud, l'Allemagne est propice à de nombreuses découvertes. *Cool Hotels Germany* vous propose un regard original sur ce pays au cœur de l'Europe en vous présentant la grande variété de ses seize états, chacun avec sa propre vie culturelle et ses paysages caractéristiques. On y retrouvera les témoins du passé : les forteresses sur le Rhin, si bien conservées qu'on s'attend à tout moment à voir un chevalier en armure passer leur porte à cheval, les châteaux et les cités médiévales avec leurs jolies maisons à colombage. Ou les méandres sinueux des rivières, les grandes forêts de montagne moyenne et les plages blanches étincelantes de la Baltique. Ce sont les paysages de l'âme allemande, qui ont inspiré les artistes dans des œuvres à la renommée internationale, du peintre romantique Caspar David Friedrich à Gerhard Richter, un des artistes les plus estimés de notre temps. Celui part à la recherche des joyaux de ce pays sera richement récompensé.

Dans des villes telles qu'Hambourg, Düsseldorf, Cologne, Francfort ou Munich, des architectures remarquables annoncent le nouveau départ vers le XXI^ème siècle. Et Berlin est en bonne route pour devenir la ville la plus *cool* du monde, surpassant toutes les autres métropoles. C'est pourquoi *Cool Hotels Germany* présente un total de huit adresses dans la capitale allemande. Hambourg a aussi beaucoup à offrir en matière de *cool*. Le *YoHo*, derrière sa blanche façade hanséatique, promet une remise à tous ses clients de moins de 26 ans. Munich, riche de ses trois pinacothèques, vous propose l'hôtel *La Maison*, à l'inspiration française, à seulement quelques pas du Jardin Anglais et du plus célèbre de tous les jardins à bières près de la Tour Chinoise.

Mais parfois les hôtels *cools* sont là où l'on s'attend le moins à les trouver. Au *Kloster Hornbach* (Monastère d'Hornbach), à la frontière française, les clients sont plongés dans une atmosphère de paix et de méditation dès qu'ils franchissent la porte du monastère. A Trier, autrefois une ville importante de l'ouest de l'Empire Romain, le *Becker's Hotel* séduit ses clients par son ambiance au style incomparable. Et avec son *Schloss der Künste* (Château des Arts), une artiste a créé un refuge spécial (et abordable) intégré dans le doux paysage du Lac de Constance. Avec ce guide dans vos bagages, partir en voyage en Allemagne signifie affûter votre regard, en voyant d'une nouvelle perspective ce qui pouvait sembler familier.

Bärbel Holzberg

## Introducción

Entre la costa del Mar del Norte y las cumbres de los Alpes hay mucho por descubrir. *Cool Hotels Germany* abre una nueva ventana al país en el corazón de Europa y nos muestra la gran diversidad presente en sus dieciséis Estados Federados, cada uno con su propia vida cultural y sus paisajes característicos. Muestra de ello son, por ejemplo, los monumentos que atestiguan el pasado: los castillos a orillas del Rin, tan bien conservados que da la impresión de que en cualquier momento podría aparecer un gallardo caballero cabalgando por sus portales; o los palacios y las ciudades medievales con las casas con fachadas entramadas extraordinariamente bien cuidadas. Testigos también son los meandros de los ríos, los extensos bosques de las montañas de mediana altura y las playas del Mar Báltico de una blancura deslumbradora. Estos míticos paisajes alemanes han inspirado a artistas a crear obras de clase mundial. Desde el romántico Caspar David Friedrich hasta Gerhard Richter, uno de los artistas más reconocidos de nuestro tiempo. Alemania es un país lleno de tesoros que vale la pena descubrir.

Las ciudades de Hamburgo, Dusseldorf, Colonia, Francfort y Munich muestran el apogeo arquitectónico del amanecer del siglo XXI. Berlín, entre todas las metrópolis internacionales, está a punto de convertirse en la ciudad de moda por excelencia. Por ello, *Cool Hotels Germany* presenta ocho direcciones en la capital alemana. En cuanto al aire innovador y moderno, Hamburgo tiene mucho que ofrecer. El *YoHo* se encuentra detrás de una fachada blanca hanseática y ofrece tarifas reducidas a los huéspedes menores de 26 años.

En Munich, la ciudad con tres pinacotecas, se encuentra *La Maison*, un hotel de encanto francés a tan sólo unos pasos del Jardín Inglés y de la más célebre de las cervecerías al aire libre en los alrededores de la Torre China.

A veces, los hoteles más carismáticos se hallan dónde nadie esperaría encontrarlos. El *Kloster Hornbach*, un monasterio cerca de la frontera francesa, depara a sus huéspedes una tranquilidad meditativa tras sus muros. En Tréveris, antiguamente una importante ciudad del oeste del Imperio Romano, el *Becker's Hotel* convence con una atmósfera muy moderna. Enclavado en el paisaje suave del Lago de Constanza, una artista creó un refugio especial pero asequible – el *Schloss der Künste* (Palacio de las Artes). Emprender un viaje por Alemania con esta guía significa agudizar la vista e incluso redescubrir con un nuevo enfoque lo que parece ya conocido.

Bärbel Holzberg

## Introduzione

Tra la costa del Mare del Nord e le cime delle Alpi del sud c'è molto da scoprire. *Cool Hotels Germany* consente di osservare da una nuova prospettiva il paese situato nel cuore dell'Europa e la sua notevole varietà, che si manifesta nelle diverse tradizioni e nei caratteristici paesaggi dei suoi sedici Länder. Testimoni del passato della Germania sono per esempio i castelli lungo il Reno, così ben conservati che da un momento all'altro ci si aspetterebbe di vedere un nobile cavaliere varcarne la porta a cavallo, i manieri e le città medievali con le loro case a graticcio tenute alla perfezione. O ancora i corsi serpeggianti dei fiumi, le vaste foreste del Mittelgebirge e le candide spiagge del Mar Baltico. E i mitici paesaggi tedeschi, che hanno ispirato artisti nella realizzazione di opere di fama mondiale, da Caspar David Friedrich, pittore romantico, a Gerhard Richter, uno degli artisti più prestigiosi del nostro tempo. Una terra, dunque, piena di tesori su cui vale la pena soffermarsi. L'architettura di città come Amburgo, Düsseldorf, Colonia, Francoforte o Monaco sottolineano il passaggio nel XXI secolo. Berlino si trova sulla giusta via per conquistarsi il titolo di città più cool tra tutte le metropoli del mondo – e proprio per questo *Cool Hotels Germany* fornisce otto indirizzi nella capitale tedesca. Anche Amburgo ha qualcosa da offrire in fatto di *coolness*: dietro la sua bianca facciata che risale all'epoca della Lega Anseatica, lo *YoHo* garantisce sconti a tutti gli ospiti sotto i 26 anni. Monaco, con le sue tre pinacoteche, offre invece *La Maison*, un albergo d'ispirazione francese situato a pochi passi dall'Englischer Garten e dalla Torre Cinese, dove si trova il Biergarten (birreria all'aperto) più famoso in assoluto.

A volte, però, gli alberghi più accattivanti si trovano proprio dove meno ci si aspetta. Nel *Kloster Hornbach*, sul confine francese, si viene circondati da una tranquillità che induce alla meditazione non appena si varcano le mura di questo monastero. A Treviri, un tempo importante città nella parte occidentale dell'Impero Romano, il *Becker's Hotel* ha un ambiente d'alta classe davvero vincente. Mentre nel dolce paesaggio del Lago di Costanza un'artista ha costruito lo *Schloss der Künste*, un vero e proprio rifugio del tutto particolare – e alla portata di tutti. Mettersi in viaggio verso la Germania con questa guida in valigia significa guardare più a fondo e, molto spesso, vedere ciò che si pensa di conoscere già da un'angolazione tutta nuova.

Bärbel Holzberg

# Cerês

Strandpromenade 24
18609 Ostseebad Binz
Phone: +49 38393 66 67 0
Fax: +49 38393 66 67 68
www.ceres-hotel.de

**Price category:** €
**Rooms:** 50 rooms and suites
**Facilities:** Restaurant and bar Negro with sea terrace
**Services:** Massages and treatments at the Senso Spa
**Located:** Cerês is located directly on the sea, it is one of the most beautiful destinations in the Baltic Sea region
**Public transportation:** 0.8 km from train station Binz
**Map:** No. 1
**Style:** Contemporary design
**What's special:** Contemporary 50 room hotel, each room has a balcony or terrace, the Cupola Suite is the highlight of all rooms, perfect for stargazing. The Senso Spa is the intimate setting for our vision of a journey towards inner balance, it offers exclusive treatments and is driven solely by the power of water.

# Kempinski Grand Hotel Heiligendamm

Prof.-Dr.-Vogel-Straße 16-18
18209 Bad Doberan
Heiligendamm
Phone: +49 38203 74 00
Fax: +49 38203 74 07 47 4
www.kempinski-heiligendamm.com

**Price category:** €€
**Rooms:** 215 rooms and suites
**Facilities:** 4 restaurants, 3 bars, sauna world, spa, pool, ballroom
**Services:** Airport shuttle, babysitting services, bridal suite, packed lunches, free wireless
**Located:** Directly at the beach of the Baltic Sea in Mecklenburg-Western Pomerania, near Rostock
**Public transportation:** Airport Rostock, train Bad Doberan
**Map:** No. 2
**Style:** Modern classic
**What's special:** This majestic building has a 3,000 m² wellness area in its own palatial space, including a Medical Spa, a separate children's area includes the Polar Bear Club with private villa and activities such as pony riding, pirate parties, and story telling.

# Jagdschloss Bellin

Am Schloss 3
18292 Bellin
Phone: +49 38458 32 20
Fax: +49 38458 32 22 0
www.jagdschloss-bellin.de

**Price category:** €
**Rooms:** 5 apartments for 6 persons, 2 apartments for 4 persons, 3 double rooms
**Facilities:** Small restaurant
**Services:** Babysitting
**Located:** Mecklenburg-Western Pomerania, close to Güstrow
**Public transportation:** 12 min to railway station Güstrow, 30 min by car to airport Rostock
**Map:** No. 3
**Style:** Modern classic
**What's special:** Hunting castle turned apartment hotel created in neo-baroque style, surrounded by 10,000 m$^2$ parkland with ponds, pavilions, mausoleum and exotic gardens, a winter garden for maximum 170 people, spa with sauna, guests can swim or sail at nearby lake.

# Clipper Elb-Lodge

Carsten-Rehder-Straße 71
22767 Hamburg
Phone: +49 40 80 90 10
Fax: +49 40 80 90 19 99
www.clipper-boardinghouses.de

**Price category:** €
**Rooms:** 57 suites
**Facilities:** Inhouse daily coffee shop, roof terrace
**Services:** Concierge, shopping, cleaning and laundry services
**Located:** Near the city center and the convention center, views over bustling Hamburg harbor
**Public transportation:** U Königstraße, Bus Stilwerk
**Map:** No. 4
**Style:** Modern classic
**What's special:** Boardinghouse for one night, one week, one month or even longer, in superb location with stunning city views, own wellness area with sauna, steam room, and solarium.

# East

Simon-von-Utrecht-Straße 31
20359 Hamburg
Phone: +49 40 30 99 30
Fax: +49 40 30 99 32 00
www.east-hamburg.de

**Price category:** €
**Rooms:** 128 rooms and suites
**Facilities:** Restaurant, bar and lounge
**Services:** Spa area with roof terrace, sauna, massage
**Located:** Near Reeperbahn
**Public transportation:** U St. Pauli, S Reeperbahn
**Map:** No. 5
**Style:** Classic elegance
**What's special:** Former iron foundry turned into award-winning designer hotel, restaurant with 230 seats serving fusion cuisine, the bar is the city hotspot, 1,000 m$^2$ fitness and wellness area.

East    35

# Gastwerk

Beim Alten Gaswerk 3/
Daimlerstraße
22761 Hamburg
Phone: +49 40 89 06 20
Fax: +49 40 89 06 22 0
www.gastwerk.com

**Price category:** €
**Rooms:** 127 rooms, 11 juniorsuites, 3 suites
**Facilities:** Riva die Bar, Ristorante Da Caio, spacious wellness area
**Services:** Babysitting on request, spa, WLAN, daily newspaper
**Located:** In the district Bahrenfeld
**Public transportation:** S Bahrenfeld, Bus Bornkampsweg
**Map:** No. 6
**Style:** Contemporary design
**What's special:** Former industrial building of old public gasworks turned into a modern design hotel, Medical Spa and health club, loft spaces with original brick walls and luxurious suites, balcony in each guest room, popular Italian restaurant.

# Monopol Hotel

Reeperbahn 48
20359 Hamburg
Phone: +49 40 31 17 71 00
Fax: +49 40 31 17 71 51
www.monopol-hamburg.de

**Price category:** €
**Rooms:** 80 rooms
**Facilities:** Bar, lounge and restaurant
**Services:** Parking, roomservice, pay-tv
**Located:** In the center of midtown's theater district, next to harbor
**Public transportation:** U St. Pauli, S Reeperbahn
**Map:** No. 7
**Style:** Modern classic
**What's special:** Historic building with 80 guest rooms, some with an antique alcove bed, complimentary mini-bar, buffet available with pastries and drinks in the lobby throughout the day.

# Madison Hotel Hamburg

Schaarsteinweg 4
20459 Hamburg
Phone: +49 40 37 66 60
Fax: +49 40 37 66 61 37
www.madisonhotel.de

**Price category:** €€
**Rooms:** 166 rooms and suites including 2 penthouses
**Facilities:** Bar, restaurant, MeridianSpa
**Services:** Private kitchen in every room, shopping service, babysitting, ice machine, laundry service
**Located:** Centrally located between the harbor, city center and Hamburg's landmark, the Michel
**Public transportation:** U Baumwall
**Map:** No. 8
**Style:** Modern classic
**What's special:** Spacious studios, lofts and suites make up this contemporary city dwelling, private kitchen in every room, offers shopping service and MeridianSpa.

# Mövenpick Hotel Hamburg

Sternschanze 6
20357 Hamburg
Phone: +49 40 33 44 11 0
Fax: +49 40 33 44 11 33 33
www.moevenpick-hamburg.com

**Price category:** €
**Rooms:** 226 non-smoking rooms and suites
**Facilities:** Cave Bar, Mövenpick Hotel Restaurant
**Services:** Solarium, sauna, sanarium, gym, parking, business center
**Located:** In the popular Schanzenpark
**Public transportation:** U, S Sternschanze
**Map:** No. 9
**Style:** Contemporary design
**What's special:** Historic 19th century water tower transformed into a 226-room hotel with panoramic views over the city and a vast popular park, includes a restaurant with adjacent terrace and the lifestyle-bar Cave in the vaults of the old tower.

# Side

Drehbahn 49
20354 Hamburg
Phone: +49 40 30 99 90
Fax: +49 40 30 99 93 99
www.side-hamburg.de

**Price category:** €€
**Rooms:** 178 rooms, 10 suites
**Facilities:** Fusion bar, fusion restaurant
**Services:** Spa treatments, room service, babysitting, concierge, cookery course
**Located:** In the city center
**Public transportation:** U Stephansplatz, Gänsemarkt
**Map:** No. 10
**Style:** Modern classic
**What's special:** Minimalist design hotel with 12-story tower of glass and natural stone, light installations in lobby, fusion restaurant with live DJs, upper floor terrace with 360-degree views of the skyline, offers spa treatments and cooking courses.

# Superbude

Spaldingstraße 152
20097 Hamburg
Phone: +49 40 38 08 78 0
Fax: +49 40 38 08 78 10 0
www.superbude.de/com

**Price category:** €
**Rooms:** 63 double rooms, 11 4-bed rooms
**Facilities:** 24 h bar, front office, sports room with Nintendo Wii, private cinema, lounge, kitchenclub
**Services:** Bicycles, skypephones
**Located:** Downtown
**Public transportation:** U, S Berliner Tor
**Map:** No. 11
**Style:** Post Modern
**What's special:** Former printing company transformed into a 6-story hotel with 74 stylish rooms, entirely new hotel concept stands for living with friends in a hotel; brown, grey, red, pink, green or blue: style up your stay!

# YoHo–the young hotel

Moorkamp 5
20357 Hamburg
Phone: +49 40 28 41 91 0
Fax: +49 40 28 41 91 41
www.yoho-hamburg.de

**Price category:** €
**Rooms:** 30 rooms
**Facilities:** Restaurant, conference rooms, ball room
**Services:** Guests under 26 years pay less
**Located:** Between the hip Schanzenviertel district and Eimsbüttel
**Public transportation:** U Christuskirche, Schlump
**Map:** No. 12
**Style:** Modern classic
**What's special:** Upscale youth hostel housed in an historic mansion with contemporary interior design from a team of young architects, it offers simple double and single rooms with designer furniture and modern amenities such as towel warmers, WLAN access and ensuite bath, inhouse syrian style restaurant Mazza.

# Hotel ÜberFluss

Langenstraße 72
28195 Bremen
Phone: +49 421 32 28 60
Fax: +49 421 32 28 67 7
www.hotel-ueberfluss.com

**Price category:** €
**Rooms**: 50 rooms and 1 suite
**Facilities:** Wellness area with pool, sauna, and fitness room, On Top Bar, Bar/Restaurant FreudenHaus
**Services:** Babysitting on request, daily newspaper, 24 h service, free Internet
**Located:** In the center of Bremen
**Public transportation**: S Am Brill, 15 min to the airport Bremen, 2 km to the main railway station
**Map:** No. 13
**Style:** Modern classic
**What's special**: Authentic designer hotel has lamps from Tom Dixon and chairs from Charles Eames, it is located seven meters above the river, with a rooftop terrace and bar offering spectacular views, unique wellness area and beauty services.

# Adlon Kempinski

Unter den Linden 77
10117 Berlin
Phone: +49 30 22 61 0
Fax: +49 30 22 61 22 22
www.hotel-adlon.de

**Price category:** €€€
**Rooms**: 304 rooms including 78 suites
**Facilities:** 2 restaurants (one of them with a Michelin star), lobby bar, terrace overlooking the Brandenburg Gate
**Services:** Concierge, limousine, 24 h butler, room service
**Located:** In the center, directly at the Pariser Platz and Brandenburg Gate
**Public transportation**: S Unter den Linden
**Map:** No. 14
**Style:** Classic elegance
**What's special**: Berlin's most prestigious hotel located adjacent to the Brandenburg Gate is a prime people watching hotspot, 6-story building has opulent interiors with wood furnishings and brocade silk fabrics.

HOTEL ADLON

Pariser
Platz

HOTEL ADLON

# Ackselhaus

Belforter Straße 21
10405 Berlin
Phone: +49 30 44 33 76 33
Fax: +49 30 44 16 11 6
www.ackselhaus.de

**Price category:** €€
**Rooms**: 35 rooms
**Facilities:** Garden, breakfast cafe Club del Mar
**Services:** Laundry, fax service, internet, multilingual staff
**Located:** Eastern part of Berlin, close to Alexanderplatz
**Public transportation**: U Senefelderplatz, S Prenzlauer Allee, Metzer Straße
**Map:** No. 15
**Style:** Contemporary design
**What's special:** 20th century colonial-style house with 35 guest suites that are divided into separate apartments with fully furnished kitchens, rooms have high ceilings and contemporary interiors designed with themes, no two rooms are similar, perfect for families.

Fax: +49 30 28 44 55 11
www.honigmond.de

**Services:** Babysitting on request, newspaper
**Located:** In the center of Berlin, 10–20 min walking distance to the main sightseeing points
**Public transportation**: U Zinnowitzer Straße, S Nordbahnhof, Bus
**Map:** No. 16
**Style:** Colonial
**What's special**: Colonial-style hotel with simple yet elegant furnishings, offers warm atmosphere and beautiful garden where you can have breakfast.

# Lux 11

Rosa-Luxemburg-Straße 9–13
10178 Berlin
Phone: +49 30 93 62 80 0
Fax: +49 30 93 62 80 80
www.lux-eleven.com

**Price category:** €
**Rooms:** 72 Apartments, 1 penthouse
**Facilities:** Restaurant, bar, Aveda Hair Spa, Ulf Haines fashion store
**Services:** Solarium, Aveda Hair Spa
**Located:** In the center of Berlin near Hackescher Markt
**Public transportation:** U, S Alexanderplatz
**Map:** No. 17
**Style:** Minimalistic
**What's special:** Situated in Berlin's hippest central district in between cool shops and trendy galleries, 72-apartment hotel is created with spacious modern interiors, public living spaces provide natural scenery with green tones and bleached wood furniture and fittings.

# THE MANDALA HOTEL

Potsdamer Straße 3
10785 Berlin
Phone: +49 30 59 00 50 00 0
Fax: +49 30 59 00 50 50 0
www.themandala.de

**Price category:** €€€
**Rooms**: 66 City/Garden Studios, 95 suites, 2 penthouses
**Facilities:** Qui Lounge, Facil Restaurant, 3 conference rooms, The Mandala Spa on 11th floor overlooking Berlin
**Services:** Concierge for theater and musical tickets, flight reservations, rent-a-car, messenger, limousine, shopping service, bread roll service with daily newspaper, laundry and ironing, public internet, babysitting
**Located:** In the heart of Berlin at the Potsdamer Platz
**Public transportation**: U, Bus, S Potsdamer Platz
**Map:** No. 18
**Style:** Cosmopolitan and individual, pure and atmospheric
**What's special**: The central location, private hotel lobby, The Mandala Spa, trendy lounge, contemporary restaurant set in the hotel garden on the 5th floor, stylish, generous suites of 40 m$^2$.

90    THE MANDALA HOTEL

# Hotel Q!

Knesebeckstraße 67
10623 Berlin
Phone: +49 30 81 00 66 0
Fax: +49 30 81 00 66 66 6
www.loock-hotels.com

**Price category:** €
**Rooms**: 77 rooms, 4 studios and 1 penthouse
**Facilities:** Q! Restaurant and Q! Memberbar (only for Hotelguests and Q! Members)
**Services:** 24 h concierge and room service, laundry, wireless Internet, spa, private cooking in the restaurant
**Located:** In the center of West Berlin, next to the shopping street Kurfürstendamm
**Public transportation**: S Savignyplatz, U Uhlandstraße
**Map:** No. 19
**Style:** Contemporary design
**What's special**: Award-winning hotel with futuristic design and room concepts, staff wears all black, 24 h concierge, the bath is the central element in each guest room, the wellness area has heated sand, a Japanese washing zone, and sauna.

# Riehmers Hofgarten

Yorckstraße 83
10965 Berlin
Phone: +49 30 78 09 88 00
Fax: +49 30 78 09 88 08
www.riehmers-hofgarten.de

**Price category:** €
**Rooms**: 23 rooms including 1 apartement suite
**Facilities:** Bar, famous restaurant e.t.a. hoffmann
**Services:** Free wireless internet, airport shuttle service, laundry, wake up service, 24 h open reception, night porter
**Located:** In Kreuzberg, surrounded by a residential area of the last century called "Riehmers Hofgarten"
**Public transportation**: U Mehringdamm
**Map:** No. 20
**Style:** Contemporary design
**What's special**: Set in a historic garden courtyard, this 23-room hotel is outfitted with furniture exclusively made for the historic Hotel Riehmers Hofgarten and original artwork from the 1990s, cuisine from the famous hotel restaurant e.t.a. hoffmann.

# Hotel de Rome

Behrenstraße 37
10117 Berlin
Phone: +49 30 46 06 09 0
Fax: +49 30 46 06 09 20 00
www.roccofortecollection.com

**Price category:** €€€
**Rooms:** 146 rooms including 43 suites
**Facilities:** Restaurant Parioli, Bebel Bar, opera court, Spa de Rome
**Services:** Babysitting, turn down service, valet parking, car park, 24 h room service, daily newspaper, shoe shining, concierge services, same day laundry
**Located:** In Berlin's historic city center on Bebelplatz
**Public transportation:** U Französische Straße
**Map:** No. 21
**Style:** Contemporary design
**What's special:** Formerly the cashier's hall of the bank, the impressive ball room features original mosaic floors and massively high ceilings, Spa de Rome offers various massages, sauna, relaxation area, fully-equipped gym, and swimming pool in the original bank vault.

# Sheraton Pelikan Hotel Hannover

Pelikanplatz 31
30177 Hannover
Phone: +49 511 90 93 0
Fax: +49 511 90 93 55 5
www.sheraton.com/hannover

**Price category:** €
**Rooms:** 147 rooms including 16 suites, 16 clubrooms
**Facilities:** Harry's New-York Bar, 5th Avenue Restaurant
**Services:** 24 h room service
**Located:** In the Pelikan quarter, next to the Eilenriede
**Public transportation:** Train Podbielskistraße, 10 min to main station
**Map:** No. 22
**Style:** Modern classic
**What's special:** Unique modern hotel in the former factory of Pelikan pen is a historic landmark that includes the spectacular Physical Park Fitness Center, spa includes sauna and steam bath, events can be arranged in the ballroom for grand occasions or the library for more intimate gatherings.

# Mauritzhof

Eisenbahnstraße 17
48143 Münster
Phone: +49 251 41 72 0
Fax: +49 251 41 72 99
www.mauritzhof.de

**Price category:** €
**Rooms**: 39 rooms including 7 suites
**Facilities:** Lounge Bar
**Services:** 24 h a day
**Located:** In the center of Münster
**Public transportation:** 350 m from the main railway station and about 30 min by taxi from the airport
**Map:** No. 23
**Style:** Modern classic
**What's special:** Modern glass structure with steel entranceway in contemporary brick building, offers library and hip lounge with red accents, all the 39 rooms are individually designed, a Mediterranean terrace café for outdoor dining in the summer.

# Hotel St. Antonius

Dagobertstraße 32
50668 Cologne
Phone: +49 221 16 60 0
Fax: +49 221 16 60 16 6
www.hopper.de

**Price category:** €
**Rooms:** 54 rooms
**Facilities:** Restaurant, bar, garden
**Services:** Non-smoking rooms and restaurant, free wireless internet access, fitness, sauna, spa, solarium, underground parking, newspaper
**Located:** Next to Cologne Cathedral and main railway station
**Public transportation:** Main station, bus
**Map:** No. 24
**Style:** Contemporary design
**What's special:** Design hotel developed into a place of international photo art, each room has its own individualized character with unique photographic art, upper floors have incredible views of the Cologne Cathedral.

# Hotel Chelsea

Jülicher Straße 1
50674 Cologne
Phone: +49 221 20 71 50
Fax: +49 221 23 91 37
www.hotel-chelsea.de

**Price category:** €
**Rooms:** 35 rooms and 3 suites
**Facilities:** Café Central
**Services:** WLAN free of charge, 24 h service
**Located:** In the city center of Cologne
**Public transportation:** S Rudolfplatz
**Map:** No. 25
**Style:** Contemporary design
**What's special:** Boutique hotel that is a popular refuge for artists and gallery owners, original pieces of art line walls, offers spacious junior suites or apartments, café & restaurant fuses art and food, seven rooftop rooms have their own terrace.

2004er
'Monastrell'
Casa Mon Frare
(Bio-Wein)
0,2    5,20

# Schloss Auel

Haus Auel 1
53797 Lohmar-Wahlscheid
Phone: +49 2206 60 03 0
Fax: +49 2206 60 03 22 2
www.schlossauel.de

**Price category:** €
**Rooms:** 3 single rooms, 12 double rooms, 6 junior suites
**Facilities:** Restaurant, clubhouse, rooms for conferences, weddings and banquetings with up to 100 people, own chapel in rococo style
**Services:** Babysitting
**Located:** 30 km from Cologne, situated in the middle of a 18 hole golf course
**Public transportation:** Airport Cologne/Bonn, ICE station Bonn/Siegburg
**Map:** No. 26
**Style:** Classic elegance
**What's special:** Late 14th century baroque-style castle with 21 fully renovated guest rooms with gorgeous furnishings, this aristocratic family-owned home is located on a huge parkland with tranquil ponds, golf course on property.

# Goldman 25hours

Hanauer Landstraße 127
60314 Frankfurt
Phone: +49 69 40 58 68 90
Fax: +49 69 40 58 68 98 90
www.25hours-hotels.com

**Price category:** €
**Rooms:** 49 individually decorated guest rooms
**Facilities:** Restaurant, bar, lounge, breakfast served
**Services:** Wi-Fi free of charge, jogging corner, iPod sound system
**Located:** Frankfurt east end, situated among design and furniture stores, creative agencies and insider clubs
**Public transportation:** U Ostbahnhof, S Osthafenplatz
**Map:** No. 27
**Style:** Eclectic design, vintage aesthetic with fancy details
**What's special:** The unique hotel is member of design hotels[TM], living room with its private terrace represents an extra communicative space, lobby, lounge, Goldman restaurant and bar are multifunctional spaces designed to meet different requirements depending on the time and needs of the day.

# Gerbermühle

Gerbermühlstraße 105
60594 Frankfurt
Phone: +49 69 68 97 77 90
Fax: +49 69 68 97 77 96 6
www.designhotels.com/
gerbermuehle

**Price category:** €€
**Rooms:** 7 single rooms, 11 double rooms, 5 suites
**Facilities:** Restaurant, winter garden with terrace, summer garden, Turmbar
**Services:** Babysitting, personal trainer on request, 24 h room service, free WLAN
**Located:** On the bank of the River Main, close to historical Frankfurt-Sachsenhausen and the city center
**Public transportation:** S, U Offenbach Kaiserlei
**Map:** No. 28
**Style:** Modern design with traditional details
**What's special:** Futuristic glass-walled dining area and minimalist lodge-style café with antlers on walls, rooms have leather furniture and glossy parquet floors, king-size bed in middle of room, 500-seat summer garden covered by ornate white umbrellas.

# The Pure

Niddastraße 86
60329 Frankfurt
Phone: +49 69 71 04 57 0
Fax: +49 69 71 04 57 17 7
www.the-pure.de

**Price category:** €€
**Rooms:** 50 rooms
**Facilities:** Pure Bar & Pure Patio
**Services:** Room service, private car park, WLAN, patio, fitness rooms, sauna, steam bath
**Located:** In the city center of Frankfurt near train station
**Public transportation:** S, U Frankfurt main station
**Map:** No. 29
**Style:** Minimalistic
**What's special:** Open minimalist space uses light and music to transform the area into a tranquil retreat for visitors, Timbertech decking has oversized Fatboy bean bags and fountains, a bar and lounge, wellness area.

# Villa Kennedy

Kennedyallee 70
60596 Frankfurt
Phone: +49 69 71 71 20
Fax: +49 69 71 71 22 43 0
www.villakennedy.com

**Price category:** €€€
**Rooms:** 134 rooms, 28 suites, 1 presidential suite
**Facilities:** JFK Bar, restaurant Gusto, Villa Spa, gym, 9 meeting rooms including a ball room
**Services:** Villa Spa has a 15 m indoor pool and treatment rooms
**Located:** Within walking distance of the Main river bank
**Public transportation:** Tram Stresemannallee, Gartenstraße
**Map:** No. 30
**Style:** Classic elegance, traditional and innovative
**What's special:** This early 19th century building is now the charming oasis of luxury and peace in the heart of Frankfurt, each of the 163 rooms are stylish and Sir Rocco's interpretation of "The Art of Simple Luxury"—a perfect place to do business and play.

# Villa Orange

Hebelstraße 1
60318 Frankfurt
Phone: +49 69 40 58 40
Fax: +49 69 40 58 41 00
www.villa-orange.de

**Price category:** €
**Rooms**: 38 rooms
**Facilities:** Bar, breakfast room with terrace, library
**Services:** Personal trainer, personal shopper
**Located:** Quiet, and yet in the heart of the city, Frankfurt's shopping area is within five min walking distance
**Public transportation:** U Musterschule
**Map:** No. 31
**Style:** Contemporary design
**What's special:** The boutique hotel Villa Orange is oriented towards guests who appreciate a comfortable, personal ambience when travelling. The personal atmosphere of the facility with its library, cosy courtyard, sunny terrace and stylish rooms make every stay something special.

# Mövenpick Hotel Frankfurt City

Den Haager Straße 5
60327 Frankfurt
Phone: +49 69 78 80 75 0
Fax: +49 69 78 80 75 88 8
www.moevenpick-frankfurt-city.com

**Price category:** €€
**Rooms**: 268 rooms, 15 superior rooms, 5 juniorsuites
**Facilities:** "All-Day" hotelbar, Mövenpick Hotel Restaurant, conference rooms
**Services:** Business center, WLAN for free, gym with panoramic view, laundry, money exchange, public parking
**Located:** In the city center, opposite the Frankfurt fair grounds, 10 min walking distance from the main railway station and to the banking district, 11 km to the airport
**Public transportation**: U, Tram Festhalle/Messe, S Messe
**Map:** No. 32
**Style:** Modern classic
**What's special**: Only 2 km from the city center, the Mövenpick Hotel Frankfurt City is both, a perfect location to visit the old town and the famous fair in Frankfurt.

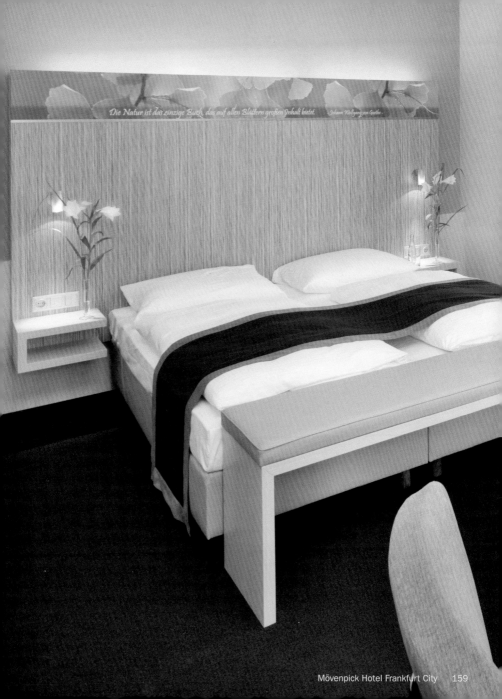

Die Natur ist das einzige Buch, das auf allen Blättern großen Inhalt bietet. *Johann Wolfgang von Goethe*

# Quartier 65

Wormser Straße 65
55130 Mainz
Phone: +49 6131 27 76 00
Fax: +49 6131 27 76 02 0
www.quartier65.de

**Price category:** €
**Rooms**: 6 rooms, non-smoking
**Facilities:** Winebar
**Services:** Welcome drink
**Located:** In the district Weisenau of Mainz
**Public transportation:** Bus Weisenauer Synagoge
**Map:** No. 33
**Style:** Minimalistic
**What's special:** Minimalist boutique hotel has only six designer rooms with a simple design concept, complimentary organic gourmet breakfast served with homemade jams, Winebar, welcome drink on arrival.

# Becker's Hotel & Restaurant

Olewiger Straße 206
54295 Trier
Phone: +49 651 93 80 80
Fax: +49 651 93 80 88 8
www.designhotels.com

**Price category:** €
**Rooms:** 9 superior double rooms, 6 junior suites, 3 suites, 14 double rooms, 3 family rooms
**Facilities:** Becker's Restaurant, Becker's Winehouse, Becker's Winebar
**Services:** Lounge library
**Located:** Only 2.5 km from the center of Trier
**Public transportation:** 30 km from the Luxembourg airport, 65 km from the Hahn airport, 3 km from the train station
**Map:** No. 34
**Style:** Natural eco flair
**What's special:** Ultra-stylish hotel built with natural materials, with a volcanic rock façade, hip restaurant and super stylish wine bar using glassware as wall art installation, lounge library.

# Kloster Hornbach

Im Klosterbezirk
66500 Hornbach
Phone: +49 6338 91 01 00
Fax: +49 6338 91 01 09 9
www.kloster-hornbach.de

**Price category:** €
**Rooms:** 34 rooms including 4 single rooms, 3 suites, and 2 maisonette suites
**Facilities:** Gourmet-Restaurant Refugium, Klosterschänke, steam bath and pool BadeLust, private registry office in the monastery's former chapel
**Services:** Babysitting, laundry, 24 h tea station, WLAN, boutique, dogs allowed
**Located:** In the center of Hornbach, close to France
**Public transportation:** 50 km to the airport Saarbrücken
**Map:** No. 35
**Style:** Contemporary design
**What's special:** This historic monastery has been transformed into a 34-room designer retreat with relaxation area BadeLust, guests can also relax in the hotel's inner courtyard and its beautiful herb garden.

# Der Zauberlehrling

Rosenstraße 38
70182 Stuttgart
Phone: +49 711 23 77 77 0
Fax: +49 711 23 77 77 5
www.zauberlehrling.de

**Price category:** €€
**Rooms:** 18 rooms including 4 suites and 1 penthouse
**Facilities:** Restaurant, private room, cookery course
**Services:** Laundry service, babysitting, rental car mini cooper, wine tastings
**Located:** In the center of midtown's theater & gallery district, next to the Altes Schloss
**Public transportation:** U Rathaus, Bus Rathaus
**Map:** No. 36
**Style:** Contemporary design
**What's special:** Located right in the heart of Stuttgart, guests can enjoy cooking courses and wine tasting, 18 stylish guest rooms including penthouse have all the most modern fixtures and high tech amenities, Mini Cooper car rental.

# Schloss Eberstein

76593 Gernsbach
Phone: +49 7224 99 59 50 0
Fax: +49 7224 99 59 55 0
www.schlosseberstein.com

**Price category:** €
**Rooms:** 14 rooms including 4 suites
**Facilities:** Gourmet restaurant, Schloss-Schänke
**Services:** Cooking classes
**Located:** In vineyards
**Public transportation:** 50 km to airport, train Karlsruhe
**Map:** No. 37
**Style:** Classic elegance
**What's special:** Gourmet restaurant on the terrace and beer garden, castle and wine estate built in the 13th century completely renovated with fourteen guest rooms including four suites with own steam room, library and relaxation garden.

Brunndobl 16
84364 Bad Birnbach
Phone: +49 8563 91 51 1
Fax: +49 8563 91 51 2
www.hofgut.info

**Price category:** €
**Rooms:** 7 theme cottages (water, tree etc.) each for two persons, 1 room for 2–4 persons in the main building
**Facilities:** Restaurant only for guests, massage cottage, sauna, wedding receptions, meeting and conference rooms
**Services:** Massages on raft floating on the lake
**Located:** Near the small city Bad Birnbach (known as a health resort) in Lower Bavaria, 40 km from Passau
**Public transportation:** Train Bad Birnbach
**Map:** No. 38
**Style:** Natural eco flair
**What's special:** Countryside hideaway perfect for uninterrupted relaxation, 2 lakes nearby, some rooms with bathtubs overlooking the valley, perfect for hiking expeditions, cooking and barista lessons, tranquil picnics.

Ledererstraße 8
80331 Munich
Phone: +49 89 24 22 49 0
Fax: +49 89 24 22 49 10 0
www.cortiina.com

**Price category:** €€
**Rooms**: 75 rooms and suites including 1 maisonette
**Facilities:** CORTIINA Bar & Lounge
**Services:** Babysitting, shoe shine service in Eduard
Meier manner, shopping service for kitchenettes
**Located:** In the center of town, between opera, Marien-
platz and the Viktualienmarkt
**Public transportation:** S, U Marienplatz or Isartor
**Map:** No. 39
**Style:** Contemporary design, modern art collection
**What's special:** Some of the 75 rooms have a private
entrance and state-of-the-art kitchenettes, stylish court-
yard and bar, classical English afternoon tea served on
exquisite Nymphenburg china during the winter season,
rooftop sun terrace, pure rubber mattresses fitted with
unbleached cotton sheets.

# Hotel La Maison

Occamstraße 24
80802 Munich
Phone: +49 89 33 03 55 50
Fax: +49 89 33 03 55 55 5
www.hotel-la-maison.com

**Price category:** €
**Rooms**: 31 rooms
**Facilities:** Bar and restaurant
**Services:** Babysitting, leave and go service for regular customer
**Located:** In the center of Schwabing, close to the English Garden
**Public transportation:** U Münchner Freiheit
**Map:** No. 40
**Style:** Contemporary design
**What's special:** Uniquely decorated guest rooms and public spaces with designer furnishings, offers picnic service in the English Garden, trendy dining area, heated floors in bathrooms.

# Hotel Opera

St. Anna-Straße 10
80538 Munich
Phone: +49 89 21 04 94 0
Fax: +49 89 21 04 94 77
www.hotel-opera.de

**Price category:** €€
**Rooms:** 25 rooms
**Facilities:** Restaurant Gandl, hotel bar, reception 24 h, safe, breakfast room, conference room for max 8 persons, quiet garden
**Services:** Room service on request
**Located:** In the heart of Munich
**Public transportation:** U Lehel, S Marienplatz
**Map:** No. 41
**Style:** Classic elegance
**What's special:** All 25 guest rooms individually furnished with antiques and rich fabrics, customized gourmet offerings in restaurant, private garden, French doors open to balconies in some rooms, delicatessen and fine wine store on premises.

# Mandarin Oriental, Munich

Neuturmstraße 1
80331 Munich
Phone: +49 89 29 09 80
Fax: +49 89 22 25 39
www.mandarinoriental.com

**Price category:** €€€
**Rooms**: 73 rooms, 48 luxuriously appointed rooms, 25 elegant suites
**Facilities:** Restaurant Mark's, with a star from guide Michelin, Mandarin Bar
**Services:** Chauffeur driven car service, car hire, dry cleaning, babysitting, 24 h room service, concierge
**Located:** City center, close to Viktualienmarkt
**Public transportation:** U Marienplatz
**Map:** No. 42
**Style:** Contemporary design
**What's special:** Award-winning hotel housed in 19th century national heritage building, personalized service, rooms with specially crafted furniture and antiques, some with private terraces.

# Bayerischer Hof

Promenadeplatz 2–6
80333 Munich
Phone: +49 89 21 20 0
Fax: +49 89 21 20 90 6
www.bayerischerhof.de

**Price category:** €€€
**Rooms**: 373 rooms including 60 suites
**Facilities:** Blue Spa with pool, saunas, fitness room, 6 bars, 3 restaurants: Palais Keller, Trader Vic's, Garden restaurant, breakfast room, bars, 40 conference rooms, entertainment, ball room for up to 2,500 guests
**Services:** Internet, disabled facilities, business center
**Located:** In the city center of Munich
**Public transportation:** S, U Marienplatz, S, U Odeonsplatz
**Map:** No. 43
**Style:** Classic elegance, contemporary cosmopolitan flair
**What's special:** Privately managed, internationally awarded luxury hotel known for its elegant flair, personal service, cosmopolitan VIP guests, design by Andrée Putman, lounge with fireplace, panorama terrace overlooking the rooftops of Munich's old center, Night Club with live jazz program.

# Öschberghof

Golfplatz 1
78166 Donaueschingen
Phone: +49 771 84 0
Fax: +49 771 84 60 0
www.oeschberghof.com

**Price category:** €
**Rooms:** 56 double rooms and 17 single rooms
**Facilities:** Hotel restaurant, Fair-way Bar, Restaurant Hexenweiher, 9 conference rooms, 2 golf courses
**Services:** Bike rental, transfer to the airport, golf equipment rental, pro shop, cosmetic studio, beauty hair
**Located:** At the door to the Black Forest between Freiburg im Breisgau, Zurich and Stuttgart
**Public transportation:** Transfer by taxi
**Map:** No. 44
**Style:** Modern classic
**What's special:** Located directly on golf course, spa and 1,800 m² wellness area with the latest high tech amenities, serene resort set in tranquil environment with panoramic views, impressive conference and banquet facilities.

# Schloss der Künste

Riedheimerstraße 8
88048 Friedrichshafen-Efrizweiler
Phone: +49 7544 24 21
Fax: +49 7544 96 59 25 5
www.schloss-der-kuenste.de

**Price category:** €
**Rooms:** 9 rooms
**Facilities:** Restaurant, wine cellar
**Services:** Complimentary breakfast, daily newspaper
**Located:** Close to the Lake Constance
**Public transportation:** 20 min to airport Friedrichshafen, bus Efrizweiler
**Map:** No. 45
**Style:** Classic elegance
**What's special:** Water castle from 11$^{th}$ century renovated into a stylish modern hotel that feels like a private home, nine stylish rooms designed by artist owner who is also passionate about cooking at her restaurant for her guests, romantic wine cellar for private events.

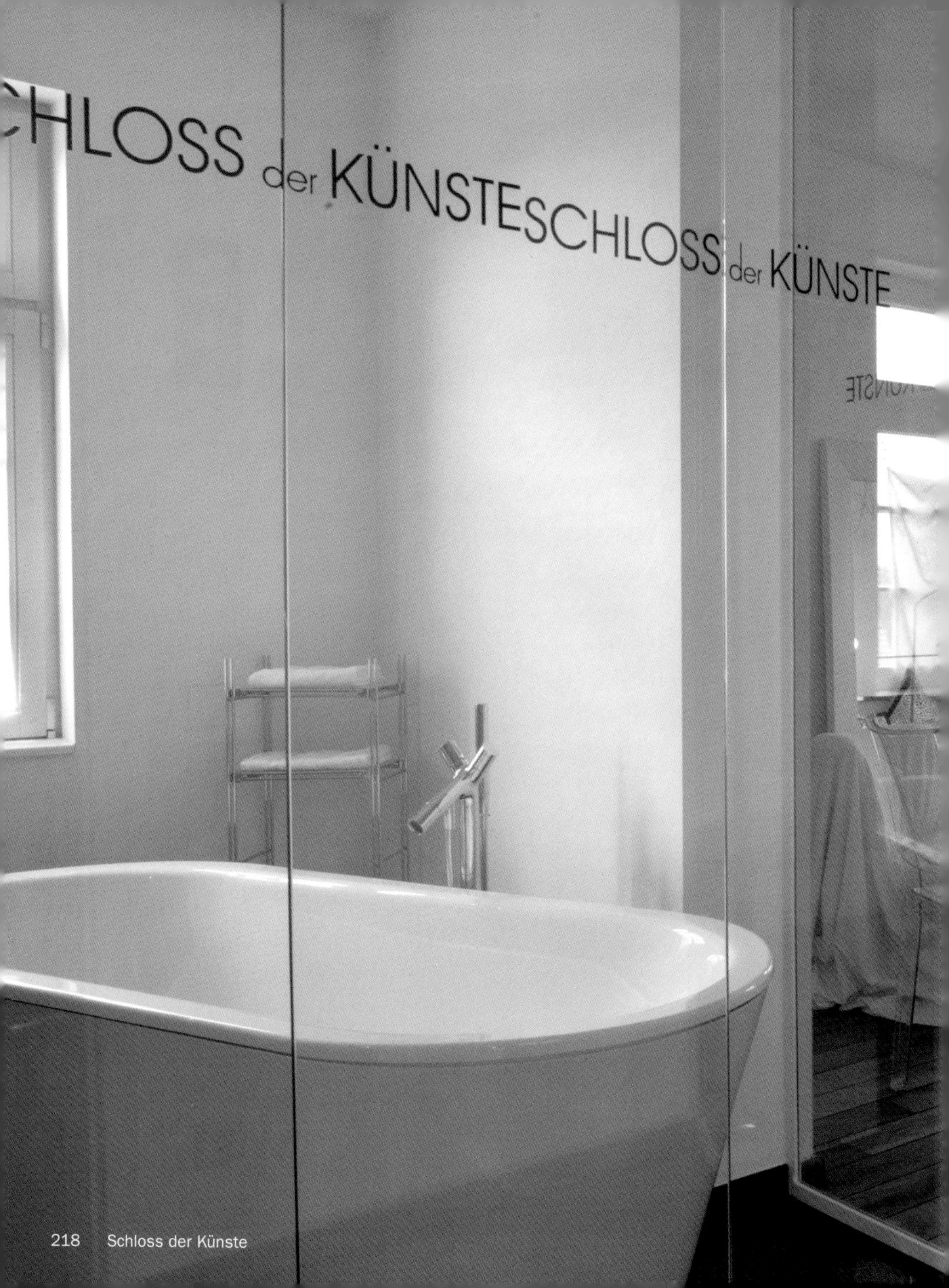

220

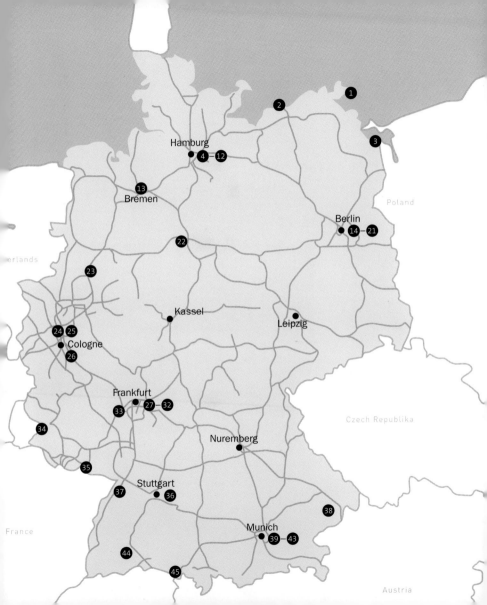

Hamburg
4—12

2

1

3

Bremen
13

Poland

Berlin
14—21

22

23

erlands

Kassel

Leipzig

24 25
Cologne
26

Czech Republika

Frankfurt
27—32

33

34

Nuremberg

35

France

Stuttgart
37  36

38

44

Munich
39—43

45

Austria

# Other titles by teNeues

# Other titles by teNeues

ISBN 978-3-8327-9206-0

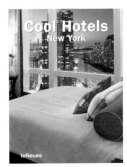

ISBN 978-3-8327-9207-7

ISBN 978-3-8327-9205-3

**Cool Hotels City:** Size: **15 x 19 cm**, 6 x 7½ in., 160 pp., **Flexicover**, c. 200 color photographs,
Text: English / German / French / Spanish / Italian

ISBN 978-3-8327-9105-6

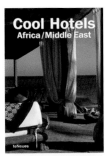

ISBN 978-3-8327-9051-6

ISBN 978-3-8238-4565-2

ISBN 978-3-8327-9134-6

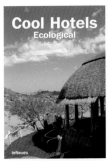

ISBN 978-3-8327-9135-3

ISBN 978-3-8327-9203-9

**Designpockets:** Size: **13.5 x 19 cm**, 5¼ x 7½ in., 400 pp., **Flexicover**, c. 400 color photographs,
Text: English / German / French / Spanish / Italian

# Other titles by teNeues

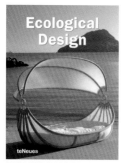

ISBN 978-3-8327-9229-9

Interior image **Ecological Design**

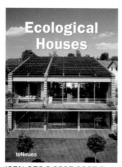

ISBN 978-3-8327-9227-5

Interior image **Ecological Houses**

ISBN 978-3-8327-9228-2

Interior image **Garden Design**

**Styleguides:** Size: **15 x 19 cm**, 6 x 7 ½ in., 224 pp., **Flexicover**, c. 200 color photographs,
Text: English / German / French / Spanish / Italian

**www.teneues.com**